Elizabeth of York
The Original Tudor Queen

K. Lee Pelt

Contents

This book is dedicated to my amazing brother, Matt.

I love to brag about the fact that he is a doctor (even though I was the first of this generation to get a graduate degree, even if it was only a Masters). He may constantly make bad Dad jokes and be way too competitive, but he is the best brother I could have asked for. He always has my back and supports me in whatever I decide to do.

Thank you, Matt. I love you!

Before We Begin...

There is a little bit of housekeeping that we need to do.

1. I use some pretty colorful language throughout this book. So if swearing is not your jam, then this may not be the book for you.

2. All of the resources that I used to research this book will be cited in "Appendix B: Sources and Further Reading." For a more in depth look at Elizabeth of York's life and the War of the Roses in general, I would highly recommend checking out some of these books.

3. All of the chapters, except for the "Introduction" and "The Legacy of Elizabeth of York", are structured in a similar way. The first part of the chapter is a section of "The Snarky Poem of Elizabeth of York". You can find the whole poem in the "Epilogue". The next section of the chapter is a short look into Elizabeth's perspective of what is happening (or the perspective of a close family member, such as her mother, Elizabeth Woodville, in

"The Pride and Joy of a New Dynasty"). The last part of each chapter goes into the historical information and all that fun stuff.

Alright, with that out of the way, I hope you enjoy Elizabeth of York's story!

Introduction

Elizabeth of York was one of those English Queens that we should know more about, but don't. She was born the firstborn heir to the York dynasty and died the first Tudor Queen. She survived the War of the Roses and came out on top when many of her loved ones (and enemies) perished throughout the war. The events she lived through are well-documented, but we have lost track of her reactions and, in some cases, her agency in those events.. This makes truly understanding who Elizabeth was (outside of the role she played as the ideal princess and then, as the perfect queen) very difficult. It does not help that there are conflicting opinions on pretty much everyone in her life.

Many of the defining events in Elizabeth's life are controversial to this day. As the older sister to the Princes in the Tower, one cannot talk about Elizabeth without talking about Richard III's ascension to the throne and the disappearance (or murder) of her brothers. The truth is that we don't know if Richard III was a nephew-killing monster, or if Dame Eleanor Butler married Edward IV, or if one of the Princes in the Tower survived and attempted to regain his throne from Henry VII. We will probably never know.

Fair warning; I, K. Lee Pelt, the Snarky History Nerd, am pretty opinionated. I know you are all very shocked by this news. I tend to give women the benefit of the doubt most of the time, especially in this time period. The people who wrote the records that we have today were men who did not like women who demonstrated that they had agency. Powerful women were often vilified for the same things that men got praised for. So, I generally take their words with a grain of salt.

Let me be frank about my opinion of the shit that went down during Elizabeth of York's life. Everybody was doing awful shit to each other. Whether they wanted power or just wanted to protect themselves and their loved ones, everyone did some pretty horrific things. There is not a single person in Elizabeth's story that was not complex and multi-facetted. Richard III was not an evil monster. He may have done some pretty evil things, but he also was trying to get rid of corruption in the English government. Elizabeth Woodville was not a power-hungry bitch. She made some pretty disastrous mistakes with severe consequences but she genuinely loved her family and did everything that she could to protect them. Basically, there is no clear villain in this story; there are just complicated people.

To be clear, there is a hero. Her name is Elizabeth of York.

One

The Pride and Joy of a New Dynasty

the nation held their breath

in the deep dark of the night

waiting...

waiting...

waiting...

"the Queen is in labor"

was the whisper on the wind.

"is it a boy or a girl?"

a pit grows in the stomach of the nation

as the night seems endless.

bright light suddenly bursts through

as word spreads

of the birth of the new heir,

Princess Elizabeth.

EXHAUSTED AND ALMOST DELIRIOUS from the delivery of her third child, she gazed down at the tiny human in her arms. Before being placed in her arms, the little girl had been cleaned and swaddled. She tried to ignore the ugly thoughts that were racing through her head that were trying to ruin this moment. Men wanted sons, not daughters, especially kings.

Fear tightened her chest as she thought about Edward's potential disappointment and anger over having a girl. As the thoughts got louder, she could taste the bile in the back of her throat. Panic was getting the best of her when the door to the dark chamber opened and her husband walked in.

She struggled to see his face through the tears welling up in her eyes. He walked forward until he stood next to the bed, staring down at the tiny person who they had made together. He seemed frozen in place for a moment before reaching out and running the back of one finger down their daughter's cheek. The baby scrunched up her nose at the feeling and he let out a wet chuckle. He then turned to look at his wife's face, a brilliant smile on his face and tears in his eyes. Elizabeth breathed a sigh of relief when she saw the utter joy in his eyes.

Elizabeth was the first-born child of Edward IV and Elizabeth Woodville. People celebrated and treated Elizabeth as a national treasure from the moment she was born. Normally, when the first-born child of a king was a girl, there was disappointment that it was not a boy. In Elizabeth's case, regardless of her gender, her birth marked the solidification of a new dynasty.

Prior to the War of the Roses, Edward IV had a claim to the throne. Was it a great one? Not so much. His claim to the throne was based on the fact that his great-great-great-grandfather on his mom's side was Lionel of Antwerp, the 2nd surviving son of Edward III, and his great grandfather on his dad's side was Edmund of Langley, the 4th surviving son of Edward III. So basically, his great-great-grandfather on his dad's side and his great-great-great-great-grandfather on his mom's side were the same person. There was way too much incest going on in the medieval era.

While the incestuous happenings of the medieval royals are interesting, the key claim that Edward IV made was that Henry VI (the king that Edward IV deposed) was descended from the 3rd surviving son of Edward III. Essentially, Edward IV's grandpa was higher in the line of succession than Henry VI's great-grandpa, which theoretically gave him a better claim to the throne. Of course, this logic completely discounts that Henry VI's father and grandfather (Henry V and Henry IV since there were only like four names in the medieval era) had been anointed Kings of England.

As a usurper, Edward IV's position as King of England was tenuous and under almost constant threat at this point. The birth of the first prince or princess was always going to be a significant event. That she was a healthy baby (and her mother survived) was seen as a sign from God that Edward IV was the rightful king and that his dynasty was secure.

Regardless of how anyone felt about Elizabeth's gender, she was the first Yorkist princess. For the first few years of her life, Elizabeth led a charmed life. Unfortunately, that world came crashing down all too soon.

Two

Betrothal Numero Uno

a political pawn,

even at the tender age of four.

her hand in marriage

treated as a consolation prize,

given to whomever whines the loudest.

the loudest lord of them all,

the man who slaughtered her family

wins the prize...

at least for today.

A WAY FROM THE ROYAL nursery at Sheen Palace, the four-year-old girl could not help but look around in awe at the splendor of the Royal Court. She had been here for some time now, but the sight of the celebrating men and women dancing and swaying around the room was mesmerizing to the young girl. She held her caretaker's, Lady Margery's, hand as they walked to the private room where the royal family met each night when they were all at court.

Tonight, the young girl was to meet with her parents without her sisters. All the attention would be on her as she recited the Book of Psalms for the King and Queen for the first time. The four-year-old overheard Lady Margery telling another woman that she needed to prove that she was old enough to be betrothed while they were still at Sheen Palace, where the princesses normally lived. Apparently, there had been some trouble with one of her older cousins and her father needed to give him something so that he would calm down. She had to prove herself to help her father.

The girl trembled with nerves as they entered the room. With a gentle push from Lady Margery's hand between her shoulder blades, she approached the King and Queen and knelt before them. Elizabeth looked up from she knelt before her parents and recited the Book of Psalms flawlessly.

While Elizabeth's birth (and survival as many children did not live to adulthood during this period of time) was a very good thing for Edward IV's reign, it did not take long for shit to hit the fan. England had just fought a civil war. Henry VI (the deposed king who had some major mental health concerns and was pretty much constantly delusional) was still alive and in Edward IV's custody. Margaret of Anjou, Henry VI's wife and queen, had fled to France with their son, Edward of Lancaster, Her cousin was the King of France and sided with Henry VI, making Margaret and Edward of Lancaster huge threats to Edward IV. Even without any in-fighting between the Yorkist faction, Edward IV's reign was one wrong move away from collapsing around him.

The implosion of the Yorkist faction was unfairly blamed on Elizabeth Woodville, Edward IV's wife and Elizabeth of York's mother. As a Lancastrian widow whose father was not noble born, Elizabeth Woodville was not considered an appropriate choice of bride for the King of England. Because of her lack of status and multitude of siblings, Edward IV gave titles, marriages and land to her siblings in order to raise her family to a more appropriate status for the Queen's family. Many of Edward IV's supporters had expected to receive these gifts as thanks for their support and it really pissed them off that

Lancastrians received the gifts instead. The biggest mistake that Edward IV made was with Richard Neville, Earl of Warwick.

Warwick (most often called "the Kingmaker") had been Edward IV's primary supporter. In fact, he had been the primary supporter of Richard of York, Edward IV's father, who had been brutally executed during one of the early battles of the War of the Roses.

Warwick made himself the power behind the throne after the Lancastrians were overthrown (the first time). He was Edward IV's second in command. Frankly, Warwick thought his shit did not stink. At the time of Edward IV's marriage, Warwick was negotiating a betrothal between Edward IV and Bona of Savoy (the French king's sister-in-law). In fact, Edward IV did not reveal his marriage until negotiations were finished and all that was needed was for Edward IV to approve the match. Many believed that this very public humiliation was one of the primary reasons why Warwick betrayed Edward IV.

Warwick began working behind the scenes to overthrow Edward IV. He colluded with Edward IV's brother, George of Clarence, to make Clarence king. Their first act of open defiance was the marriage between Clarence and Isabel Neville, Warwick's oldest daughter. This spiraled into a full on revolt, in which Warwick murdered Elizabeth Woodville's father and brother. And no, I do not mean that they died in battle. Warwick illegally put them on "trial" and executed them for treason.

He took Edward IV captive and attempted to rule on his behalf. This failed epically and Edward IV returned to the throne soon after.

In an attempt to make nice with Warwick, Edward IV betrothed his oldest daughter, Elizabeth, to George Neville, Warwick's nephew and male heir. This was essentially putting a Band-Aid over a gaping wound. This betrothal did not appease Warwick's ambitions and Elizabeth Woodville hated it. After all, her husband had just promised to marry her daughter to the nephew of the man who murdered her father and brother. This fragile peace did not last long, and Warwick began plotting with Clarence, once again.

Three

Sanctuary Part 1

all at once,

everything changed.

the world that was once so big

shrunk to three borrowed rooms.

everything was taken away

all at once.

O N ANY OTHER DAY, the ride on the barge down the Thames River to Westminster Abbey would have been enjoyable. Right now, the young girl bravely tried to face her fear of the dark that seemed to envelop her as they slowly glided down the river. She shivered as cold air hit her face. Her caretaker had bundled her up after dragging her from her bed in the middle of the night, so her face was the only thing that was exposed. However, the cold seemed to seep into her bones and down to her toes. It felt like she would never get warm again.

She looked at her mother, hoping to find some sort of comfort in her, but the look of unadulterated terror on her mother face made her pause. Her mother sat stiffly, her shaking hands cradling her very pregnant belly. The young girl could almost make out the tears in her mother's eyes, despite the pitch black darkness that surrounded them. Elizabeth knew, right then, that something was very, very wrong.

Despite Edward IV's attempts to appease Warwick while also keeping his power in check, Warwick was not satisfied. He had had a taste of power that was well above his station (which makes his bitching about the "upstart" Woodvilles were reaching above their station extremely hypocritical). To be frank, Warwick wanted to be king. This was pretty much not possible, as while his aunt (Cecily Neville) was Edward IV's mother, the closest hereditary link to the throne was his grandmother, Joan Beaufort. Joan Beaufort was the daughter of John of Gaunt and Kathryn Swynford. John of Gaunt was one of Edward III's sons, but more importantly (for this rant at least), he was Henry IV's father, AKA the OG Lancaster King. Trying to claim the throne through his Lancastrian grandmother would not have been a good look for the Yorkist "Kingmaker" (AKA Warwick). Also, there was the glaring fact that Joan Beaufort was born out of wedlock and was later legitimized once her parents got married many years later.

Back to my original point, the likelihood that Warwick could claim the throne in his own right was about the same as a snowball's chance in hell. So, he needed a puppet king. He had already tried and failed (epically) to imprison Edward IV and rule on his authority. Placing Clarence on the throne and ruling through him as his father-in-law was a possibility. However, it was probable that Clarence would rebel against Warwick's control, much in the same way that Edward IV had. With Yorkist options looking not great (not that he clued in his ally, Clarence), he turned to the Lancastrians. After all, this whole mess started because Henry VI was an incompetent ruler who others used for their own personal gain.

So Warwick fled to France with his family, including Clarence, and made a deal with Margaret of Anjou, the deposed Queen Consort (AKA Henry VI's wife). To finalize the deal, he married his youngest daughter, Anne, to Edward of Lancaster (Henry VI and Margaret of Anjou's only child and the Lancastrian heir to the throne). Warwick, then, departed from France with his new Lancastrian allies and chased Edward IV out of England.

With the Lancastrian invasion and Edward IV's flight to Burgundy, it suddenly became very dangerous for Elizabeth of York and her family. Aside from being the now deposed King's family and heirs, Warwick had a significant personal grudge against anyone related to the Woodvilles (AKA Elizabeth's entire maternal side of the family) and the last time he gained control of England, he murdered Elizabeth's grandfather and uncle. In fear for their lives, Elizabeth Woodville, Jacquetta of Luxembourg, and the York princesses were smuggled out of the Tower of London and claimed Sanctuary in Westminster Abbey.

Claiming Sanctuary in a church was a loophole that people used to escape the law. There were essentially two sets of laws: Church law and the law of the land (in this case, England). If you were in trouble with the law of the land, you could enter any church and ask for Sanctuary. As long as you remained within the Church grounds, the local law enforcement could not arrest you. The minute you left the Church grounds, you were fair game. Of course, Sanctuary was essentially symbolic and law enforcement (or your political enemies) could storm the Church and forcibly remove you, but it was not in good taste.

In the royal family's case, while they had not been accused of treason yet, there was ample reason to believe that Warwick would have had them tried and executed for treason, if he caught them. After all, the last time he had rebelled, he had done exactly that to the Queen's father and brother. With Warwick marching on London and Elizabeth Woodville heavily pregnant, seeking Sanctuary in Westminster Abbey was the best option.

The Abbot gave the royal family three rooms in his personal quarters, instead of having them stay with the other people seeking Sanctuary. The Queen ended up giving birth to the long awaited male heir while they were in Sanctuary.

To say that this period of Elizabeth's life was traumatizing was an understatement. Although she was only four years old and would not have had clear memories of these months, she was old enough to be aware of the tension and fear that consumed the adults around her. The disruption of her routine of traveling to court and staying at Sheen Palace was alarming enough without being close quarters with her mother while she gave birth. Luckily, this time, she was able to return to her normal life when her father put down the rebellion.

Four

Lancasters Be Gone!

her knight in shining armor

came back to save the day

riding in on his white steed.

it was easy to ignore

the stains of blood

that he tried to wash away

when the shining light of freedom

hit her eyes once more.

her daddy came home

and everything would be okay...

A FTER SEVERAL LONG, DREARY months spent hidden away in the three small rooms in Westminster Abbey, the young girl walked back into the familiar Palace of Westminster, surrounded by her family. She eagerly looked up at the faces of the people that they passed on the way to her father. The palace was crowded with servants, nobles and knights. Many of their faces were familiar, although she struggled to place names and families to them, while others were entirely new. She had grown accustomed to only seeing only the faces of her female relatives, the few servants who tended to the royal family and the holy men who tended to the souls of all those who came to the Abbey. Being amongst so many people was exhilarating and exhausting all at the same time.

One face stood out from all the others. At first, the little girl did not recognize him, although he seemed familiar. It had been months since she had seen him last. Recognition hit all at once. She forgot all of her courtly manners as utter joy filled her body as she began to run towards him. He knelt down on one knee and opened his arms. She flung herself at him as he caught her and held her close. She buried her tiny face into his neck as she began to cry. He smelled like the incense that the holy men constantly lit in the Abbey mixed with sweat. Elizabeth of York could not say why she was weeping because all she could think about was that her daddy was home and everything would be okay again.

ONE OF THE FIRST things that Edward IV did upon returning to England, even before he completely defeated the Lancastrians, was to liberate his wife and children from Sanctuary. He secured his family in the Tower of London and spent a few days with them before marching to meet Warwick in battle. Edward IV was determined to remove the threats to his throne and family. This time, there would be no attempts at reconciliation between the two sides, (unless, of course, you were his brother, as George of Clarence slithered away with a mere slap on the wrist).

In his desperation to end the Lancastrian threat, Edward IV made a very controversial decision that would eventually come back to haunt Elizabeth of York. After the Battle of Tewkesbury (which was the battle where Edward IV defeated the Lancastrian line through Henry VI), many Lancastrian nobles fled to Tewkesbury Abbey and claimed Sanctuary. Two days after the end of the battle, Edward IV had the nobles dragged out of Tewkesbury Abbey and executed, violating Sanctuary. In this moment, all that mattered was getting rid of his enemies and he seemingly forgot that his wife and children had just been saved by declaring Sanctuary at Westminster Abbey.

With Warwick, Edward of Lancaster, and the majority of Lancastrian supporters dead, there was one significant player that was left, Henry VI. You know, the former king who was currently in Edward IV's custody back in London. After violating Sanctuary, one would have expected that Edward IV's tactics to get rid of Henry VI would have been brutal. The official story was that after hearing about the death of his son, he died of a broken heart. However, the rumor was that Edward IV had him killed and that the future Richard III was involved in the assassination. The Lancasters had lost their teeth and the in-house traitors had been purged. Or had they?

Five

The Problem With Uncle George

but was it really all hunky dory dory?

were all the villains of this story

washed away with

the blood of Teweksbury?

nah.

King Eddie stuck his head in the sand

as Uncle Georgie Porgie danced on graves;

cackling in the moonlight.

A T THE NEWS, HER mind went blank. Terror. Complete and utter terror was the only emotion she could process. The only time in her life that she remembered feeling this way was years before. Confined to the three room apartment at Westminster Abbey, she could remember the dark and her mother's screams of pain as she gave birth in the room next door. The pit in her stomach seemed to grow with the shadow monsters as they danced on the walls of the small room. That had been the last time that she felt this fear tremble through her body.

At this moment, years later and on the cusp of womanhood, she was taken back to that horrible place in her mind. How could she not? There was a threat against her father and brother, she was told. A threat that involved her uncle; the same uncle that had threatened her father the last time. It took all her focus to keep her face from showing the abject terror that she was feeling. After all, she was Princess Elizabeth. Showing fear was not an option.

~~>>>> <<<<~

George, Duke of Clarence, was a selfish asshole. He spent his life scheming for more power, money, and land, never satisfied with his position in life. And he had a really good position. With his older brother as king, he was second in line to the throne, at least until Edward IV started having children. George was directly involved with almost every major rebellion that Edward IV was faced with in the early years in his reign. And that was not counting all of the times that George directly defied Edward IV.

Let's take a look at only some of George's dickish behavior:

- He spread rumors that Edward IV was illegitimate, disparaging his mother's reputation in the process.

- He married Isabella Neville, despite Edward IV flat out declaring that George was not allowed to marry Isabella Neville.

- He teamed up with Warwick to incite a rebellion on the promise that Warwick would overthrow Edward IV and place George on the throne.

- He only switched back to Edward IV's side of the rebellion when it became clear that Warwick put his eggs in the Lancastrian basket, not George's.

- He attempted to marry Mary of Burgundy, which messed up the Treaty of Picquigny (for more information, check out the chapter called "Future Queen of France...Maybe?).

- He fought with Richard III over their mother-in-law's inheritance so much that Edward IV was forced to declare her dead (even though she was very much alive) so that George and Richard III could split her estate.

- He accused Elizabeth Woodville of poisoning Isabella Neville when she actually died in childbirth.

- He conspired to use sorcery against Edward IV and Edward V.

So basically, George, Duke of Clarence, was the shittiest brother, uncle, and son ever (slight exaggeration but also kind of true). The only reason why he lasted as long as he did was because Edward IV was his brother. And despite how awful George was, Edward IV did not want to execute his brother.

This ended when George conspired to use sorcery against Edward IV and his son Edward V. The fact that he was suspected of being involved was something that Edward IV could have ignored; however, George made a fatal mistake. He defended his conspirators in front of the Privy Council.

This blatant attempt to harm the King of England and his heir sealed George's fate. While Cecily Neville, Edward IV's mother, pleaded with her son to spare George one more time, Elizabeth Woodville argued that enough was enough. The man had threatened their son and the heir to the throne. She feared for the safety of her children should he live. Ultimately, Edward IV sided with Elizabeth Woodville. George, the Duke of Clarence, was put on trial in front of Parliament and condemned as a traitor. The only concession that Edward IV made for Cecily's sake was that George was spared a traitor's death and his execution was private, instead of a public spectacle.

At this point, Elizabeth of York was old enough to understand what was happening. Her uncle had tried to hurt her father and brother. This moment taught Elizabeth two very important lessons that she held onto for the rest of her life: sometimes, you cannot trust even your family, and your spouse and children come before everyone else.

Six

Future Queen of France... Maybe?

the golden princess

is to be the next Queen of France,

as long as fickle foes stay true.

but alas, they rarely do.

the Princess may be the Dauphine for now,

but a better offer may come through.

S HE COULD NOT REMEMBER a time when she was not la
Dauphine. Logically, she knows that there was a point
when she was merely a Princess of England, but that was so long

ago that she could barely remember. She spent years preparing to be the next Queen of France and it was finally time for her to step into that role. Her head in the clouds, the young woman glided around the palace as though she were walking on air. Her joy was infectious as any day now, her father would get word from the French king that it was time for Elizabeth of York to move to her new home. Any day now, her life was going to begin.

Like entirely way too many of his ancestors, Edward IV decided that England was not enough land for him, so he tried to invade France. Not a great idea, since the main complaint against his predecessor was how badly he fumbled the war in France. Edward IV's invasion was a major flop. His "allies", Burgundy and Brittany, both deserted him and backed the French king. Since there was no way that Edward IV could win a full out war with France on his own, he met with Louis XI of France and signed the Treaty of Picquigny.

Part of this treaty was a marriage agreement (because what else was Edward IV going to do with his daughters other than sell them to the highest bidder). According to the treaty, Elizabeth of York and Dauphin Charles, the son of Louis XI, would marry when they came of marriageable age (which was, of course, way too young). This was a huge moment as there had never before been an agreement for an English princess to potentially become the Queen of France.

This agreement started unraveling when George the Jerk started plotting to marry Mary of Burgundy. Louis XI saw this play as England trying to ally itself with Burgundy against France. Clearly, he had not been paying attention to the shitstorm that was English politics for the last decade. The very last person that Edward IV would send to seal an alliance with Burgundy was George. Edward IV saw this move for what it was; George was trying to get more power to launch another coup against Edward IV. While George's nefarious plans did fall through, Louis XI saw this as a betrayal and started to look elsewhere for the next Queen of France.

It definitely did not help that when Mary of Burgundy did get married, she and her husband, eventual Holy Roman Emperor Maximilian I, immediately rebelled. Mary's father, Charles the Bold, made catastrophic errors during his reign, which led to Louis XI taking much of Burgundy and dismantling the territory. Louis XI expected the rebellion so when George was in the running to marry Mary, Louis XI took it as a sign that Edward IV was not going to hold up his end of the treaty.

Edward IV tried to convince Louis XI that he was all in. He ignored Mary's plea for aid. He sent ambassador after ambassador to France, practically begging Louis XI to keep his end of the deal. As the months passed, it was clear that Louis XI was just stringing Edward IV along. He had no intention of marrying his son to Elizabeth of York; however, with Burgundy in revolt, it was highly likely that Edward IV would back Burgundy if Louis XI pissed him off.

Over the next few years, the kings of France and England continued to play a cat and mouse game while Elizabeth waited patiently for word on when she would go to France to marry the Dauphin. Edward IV threatened to back Burgundy. Louis XI basically ignored him until Burgundy won a battle. Then, the French king gave in and paid part of the dowry per the agreement to appease Edward IV. Louis XI got comfortable and reached out to Scotland about a potential marriage alliance. Edward IV found out and shut it down. Burgundy increased their pleas to Edward IV. In response, France sent more money to continue to string the king of England along and keep him out of the fight. This pattern went on and on with Louis XI and Edward IV trying to out political maneuver the other.

This game came to an abrupt end with the Treaty of Arras. With the untimely death of Mary of Burgundy, Louis XI was able to gain enough support from the Burgudian people to end the Burgundian rebellion and secure a marriage between the Dauphin and Mary's daughter, Margaret of Burgundy. When Edward IV learned of the new treaty, he flew into a rage and wanted to invade France in revenge. As Elizabeth of York was now a teenager, he immediately began looking for another match for her. Interestingly enough, he began negotiations with Margaret Beaufort, mother of Henry Tudor, the remaining Lancastrian threat. Unfortunately, everything fell apart rather spectacularly before Edward IV could secure Elizabeth of York's future.

Seven

The Death of A King

with the removal

of one single card,

the Tower of Cards

that the princess lives in

comes crashing

down

down

down.

TO THIS DAY, SHE could not tell you who gave her the horrible news. At first, the words did not even make sense.

They jumbled in her mind as up became down. Then, once she registered what they meant, she did not believe them. How can her father, so full of life, be gone. It just was not possible. Yes, he had been sick but he was going to get better. He had to get better.

But, then reality hit, as one single tear escaped down her cheek. He was gone. Her father. Her knight in shining armor. Her king. He was gone. Suddenly, her chest began to tighten and she could not get air. She heard someone let out a heartbreaking cry and then gasping sobs. It took several minutes to realize that the awful noise was coming from her, as the sobs overtook Elizabeth of York. Her father was dead.

Edward IV died suddenly at forty-one, leaving his twelve year old son, Edward V, as his heir. England was once again thrown into turmoil, as nothing good ever came from a child king. As the remaining York brother, Richard III was named Lord Protector in Edward IV's will. While Richard III was certainly the most loyal sibling that Edward IV had, he had spent much of the last part of Edward IV's reign as the crown's representative in the north and had not spent a lot of time at court. He barely knew his nieces and nephews, but held a distinct dislike for the Woodvilles. There were a few reasons for this. Richard III had once been close to his brother, George, and like many other

Woodville haters, overlooked the treason aspect of his death and laid the blame at Elizabeth Woodville's feet. The other reason was his wife, Anne Neville.

Anne Neville was a complex historical figure, which unfortunately, not much was known about her. As the youngest daughter of Warwick (remember him? The original Woodville hater...), she was definitely not a fan of Elizabeth Woodville. At the height of her father's rebellion, she married Edward of Lancaster, Henry VI's only child, and became the Princess of Wales. After his untimely death in battle not long after their marriage, she lived with her sister, Isabella Neville, and brother-in-law, the infamous George of Clarence until she married Richard III. Growing up surrounded by two of the biggest Woodville haters and watching their falls from grace while the Woodvilles continued to thrive did not improve Anne's opinion of Elizabeth Woodville.

Without a doubt, the distrust and dislike were mutual. Anne's father had, after all, murdered Elizabeth Woodville's brother and father during his first rebellion. And of course, the whole second rebellion forced her to give birth to the next king while hiding in sanctuary. Elizabeth Woodville took one look at this state of affairs and immediately made moves to consolidate her power in order to protect her family.

In the case of a child king, whoever had custody of the king had the power. Edward V lived separately from the rest of the royal children, as he was the heir to the throne. Not trusting anyone outside of her family, she arranged for her brother, the current Earl Rivers, and her son from her first marriage, Sir Richard Grey, to run his household while Edward V was in his minority. It was these two men, along with two thousand troops, that attempted to escort Edward V to London for his coronation.

Anticipating the Woodvilles' tactics, Richard III, with Henry Stafford, Duke of Buckingham, intercepted Edward V at Stony Stratford. Richard III arrested many of Edward V's escort, including Earl Rivers and Sir Richard Grey. Edward V protested against their arrest, but Richard III held firm. While the news that Richard III now had custody of Edward V and arrested her uncle, Earl Rivers, and her half-brother, Sir Richard Grey was nerve-wracking to Elizabeth of York, the deafening silence from the nobility at the treatment of two members of the king's family showed her just how little support her family had. And during the War of the Roses, being royalty with little to no support amongst the nobles was very dangerous.

Eight

Sanctuary Part 2

her world shrunk

from palaces and parties

to a few rooms and prayers.

so familiar but yet so foreign.

the wails that echoed through the rooms

had once upon a time belonged to her brother

now emerged from her mother.

there would be no white knight this time.

there would be no hope this time.

ER MOTHER'S HEART-WRENCHING SOBS would haunt her until the day that she died. Watching her mother break sent a shiver of fear down her spine. For years, she had never seen her mother cry, at least, not like this. Even when facing down the haters, like Uncle George, her mother did not flinch. But, looking down at her regal mother, sitting on the floor, wailing like a child, she felt true fear for the first time in years. Emotion began to well up within her as though it would burst uncontrollably from her at any moment.

Then she saw her little brother's face. He was trying desperately not to cry. His whole body seemed to shake with the effort. Not far from him were their sisters, who were trying to hide their tears. In that moment, she knew what she had to do. She straightened her shoulders and pushed down her tears. She moved towards her siblings and urged them gently into the other room, away from their hysterical mother. Elizabeth of York spent the next several hours comforting and playing with her younger siblings as her mother's wails faintly echoed through the room. She could not take away her mother's grief and fear, but she could help by caring for the young ones, while her mother could not.

With no one to turn to for aid and feeling the walls closing in on her, Elizabeth Woodville packed up her remaining family not in the clutches of Richard III and fled to Westminster Abbey. John Eastney, Abbot of Westminster and godfather to Edward V, welcomed them with open arms and gave them the same suite of rooms that they stayed in the first time.

While the first stay in Westminster Abbey had been scary for Elizabeth of York as a toddler, this stay was petrifying. As a teenager, Elizabeth of York understood what was happening and the very real danger that her family faced. This time, there was no possibility of her father riding to the rescue as he had done over a decade before. Her mother was inconsolable and convinced that Richard III meant to kill them all. It did not help that, in Elizabeth's eyes, Richard III had proven that he could not be trusted, much like George, Duke of Clarence. As the unofficial Lord Protector, he had already arrested her uncle and brother and gained custody over her younger brother. It did not help matters that even before Richard III entered the city, Westminster Abbey was surrounded by his troops, keeping Elizabeth and her family prisoner.

During Elizabeth's last stay at Westminster Abbey, the sanctity of sanctuary (say that five times fast) held a lot more weight than it did this second time around. In fact, it had been Edward IV who violated the sanctuary of the Abbey of Tewkesbury in an effort to rid England of the Lancasters. The violation of sanctuary by the King of England set a dangerous precedent that put his wife and children in direct danger after his death.

As if matters could not get any worse, due to being in sanctuary, Edward IV's will could not be executed and Elizabeth and her family were left penniless. They were completely reliant on the Abbot of Westminster for both their safety and their living expenses. In comparison to the extravagant lifestyle that Elizabeth was used to at court, living in sanctuary and at the generosity of the abbot was a shocking change for her that only seemed to get worse as events unfolded.

Having his sister-in-law and nieces and nephew flee into sanctuary was a really bad look for Richard III. While many may not have liked the Woodvilles, Edward V was the rightful heir to the throne and Richard III's aggressiveness unsettled many nobles, especially William Hastings, Edward IV's Lord Chamberlain. An enemy of the Woodvilles, Hastings first aligned with Richard III, believing he was the best regent for the young king. However, he soon came to regret his allegiance.

Nine

A Coup In The Making

the countdown to the big day begins.

the coronation should be the event of the decade.

freedom seems so close

yet so far away.

dark rumblings bubble up

From below the surface.

a volcano of chaos began to erupt.

lava slowly dripping down the side of the mountain,

inching closer and closer.

L ORD HASTINGS HAD NEVER been her favorite person. He had been her dad's right hand man and his best friend, so he was a constant presence in her life for as long as she could remember. The issue always was that he hated her mom and the feeling was mutual. She could not remember a time when the two had not been feuding. Regardless of how important Lord Hastings was to her dad, her loyalty was always going to be with her mom. Always.

When the news came that Lord Hastings had been executed for treason, surprisingly, her eyes filled with tears. Another constant in her young life had been ripped away. Another connection to her father was gone. It hit her suddenly that he had been executed for treason. The last person that Elizabeth of York would have thought would commit any treasonous act would be Lord Hastings. What the hell was going on?

⇝⇝ ⇜⇜

While Edward V was certainly a minor, he was old enough to weigh in on the ruling of England. With this in mind, Richard III's Lord Protector role was set to vanish upon Edward V's coronation, diminishing Richard III's power significantly. Securing his power base became his first priority and the first step was to extend his Lord Protectorship past the coronation. This was where the Regency Council for Edward V split into two factions. The pro-Edward V faction, led by Hastings, were busy organizing the coronation. The pro-Richard III faction were meeting in secret to orchestrate the Lord Protector extension.

Everything came to a head when Richard III accused Hastings of plotting against him with the Woodvilles. He claimed that Hastings was the ringleader of the plot to use witchcraft to kill him. Part of this claim was true and part of it was frankly ridiculous. In a sense, Hastings was plotting against Richard III. He was not in favor of extending Richard III's role as Lord Protector after Edward V's coronation and was working with his faction of the Regency Council to ensure that the extension did not go through. Was he planning Richard III's murder? Probably not. But was he conspiring to curb his power? Absolutely.

The Woodville part was the most ridiculous part at that time. Today, the witchcraft portion may seem ridiculous but back then, it was totally plausible. On the other hand, the idea that the Woodvilles were in a position to overthrow Richard III as Lord Protector was absurd. The former Queen and her children were hiding in Sanctuary. The other Woodvilles and their supporters were either imprisoned or in hiding. Most of the nobles had turned their backs on their plight. There was also the issue that Hastings hated the Woodvilles. Hastings's main goal was to ensure that the son and heir of Edward IV became king and that he remained a powerful noble.

Whether or not the accusations against Hastings had merit, he was swiftly arrested and executed for treason. With Hastings dead and Edward V in his custody, there was one last person that Richard III needed to gain control over before he could make his final move to take the throne.

Ten

Surrendering the Final Prince

"Uncle" Hastings was the first

taken by the lava

Uncle Anthony and Older Richard were next.

she watched, helpless, as

the stranger who was her uncle

escorted her baby brother

up the mountain

towards the lava.

T HE ARGUMENT BETWEEN HER mother and the Archbishop of Canterbury was giving her a headache. She
resisted the urge to rub her temples as the Archbishop's whining
voice grated on her last nerve. He was trying to convince them
that her baby brother would be safe with their uncle. She was
not sure if he actually believed that or if he was full of shit. After
all, their dear Uncle Richard's army was currently surrounding
the Abbey.

In the end, she knew that it did not matter if Uncle Richard
promised that baby Richard would be safe. These days, fear
seemed to be her constant companion. It reared its ugly head
when she thought of her brother she caught glimpses of the
army just waiting for the order to storm the Abbey or when she
thought about her brothers who were in his custody already.
Elizabeth of York looked at her brother while he tried desperately not to cry and tried to imprint his face, his voice, his laugh,
his... well... everything into her memory in case this was the last
time that she ever saw him.

⇥⇥⇥ ⇤⇤⇤

With the exception of Edward V and her Grey half-brothers,
Elizabeth of York grew up in the same household as her siblings.
Thomas and Richard Grey were not only older than Elizabeth,
they were also not of royal blood (as for very sexist reasons, their
mother was considered a commoner), so were not raised in the

royal nursery. Edward V, on the other hand, as the heir to the throne, was raised separately in his own household by his uncle, Anthony Woodville. By no means did this mean that Elizabeth was not close to these three brothers, but she was much closer to her sisters and youngest brother, Richard, Duke of York. As there are a lot of Richards in this story, let's call him Prince Richard.

Since Elizabeth, Prince Richard, and their sisters were with their mother in the Tower of London when Richard III took custody of Edward V, they all fled into Sanctuary. As mentioned before, this was a really bad look for Richard III. It was bad enough that the Queen Dowager and the York Princesses were hiding from the Lord Protector of England. It was so much worse that Edward V's heir (AKA Prince Richard) was hiding with them. Regardless of whether or not at this point Richard III planned to take the throne, he needed to get Prince Richard out of Sanctuary ASAP.

At this point, Richard III had made his version of diplomatic overtures to try and convince Elizabeth Woodville to come out of Sanctuary. He had been negotiating via letters since arriving in London. And while he had Westminster Abbey surrounded, at least he was not with his full army (yet). And while he had arrested her brother, Anthony Woodville, and her son, Richard Grey, he had not convicted and executed them for treason (yet). And while he had executed Hastings, her late husband's best friend and her son's (Edward V) most powerful supporter, her son was still alive and getting ready for his coronation (for now, at least). Given all of these shenanigans, it was not surprising that Elizabeth Woodville stubbornly remained in Sanctuary.

So, Richard III brought out the big guns, so to speak. His army surrounded Westminster Abbey quite menacingly. Now, twenty years ago, the army would have been viewed as an empty threat. Sanctuary was sacred and to violate that to drag out anyone, especially women and children, was super bad press. But now, there was precedent for violating Sanctuary, which was created by Edward IV, the husband and father of the people cowering from his brother in Sanctuary. Those ships and soldiers posed a very real threat to Elizabeth and her family, and they all knew it.

Then, Richard III sent in the Archbishop of Canterbury. Thomas Bourchier, to retrieve Prince Richard. Surrounded by enemies, Elizabeth Woodville reluctantly relinquished her youngest son, only after getting the promise from Brouchier that Prince Richard would be returned to her after the coronation. Elizabeth of York watched her brother leave the safety of Sanctuary. This was the last time she ever saw her baby brother.

Eleven

Princess to... Bastard?

he used treachery

when he came for the Woodvilles.

he used his authority

when he came for "Uncle" Hastings.

he used his army

when he came for her brother.

there was no one left to protect her

when they came for her name.

H ER CHEST GOT TIGHT and it became hard to breathe.
She clasped her hands in front of her so that no one

could see how hard they shook. She could feel the scream climbing up her throat, as if she had no control over her body. Rage unlike anything that she had ever felt before consumed her. She could almost see herself losing control. She wanted to throw the elegant cup of wine in front of her. She wanted to smash the plates that held the food necessary to sustain her. She wanted to scream at the top of her lungs so that everyone could know her rage.

Instead, she slowly took a deep breath. She calmly unclasped her hands and picked up the cup and took a sip of wine. It tasted like ash in her mouth but she held her composure. Tonight, she would bury her face in her pillow and scream until she cried. She could release her rage away from the judging eyes that surrounded her at all times. Now, Elizabeth of York would act as a Princess of England should. Regardless of what Uncle Richard said, she was a Princess of England, not a bastard.

❧ ❧

Within the three months since the death of Edward IV, his youngest brother, Richard III, had swiftly either removed or gained custody of all of the obstacles to him taking the throne. Whether or not that was his original intent upon leaving his holdings after hearing of his brother's sudden death, he was now in the perfect position to do so. He had the two people with a better claim to the throne than him under his "protection" in the Tower of London. The Woodvilles were either in hiding, arrested, or in Sanctuary with little to no allies. Hastings had been executed for "treason". All that was left was to make an argument for why he deserved the throne over his nephews.

The excuse he used was similar to George, Duke of Clarence's, favorite accusation against Edward IV. George used to claim that Edward IV was illegitimate, not caring that he was essentially claiming that his own mother had cheated on his father and was incredibly insulting. Richard III, on the other hand, focused on the legitimacy of Edward IV's children, not Edward IV himself. Apparently, prior to marrying Elizabeth Woodville, Edward IV entered into a pre contract of marriage with Eleanor Talbot, an English noblewoman.

Now, why did this "pre contract" matter? Nobles broke betrothals all the time, right? A pre-contract was considered the equivalent to a marriage, just without all of the hoops that the Catholic Church wanted people to go through. It took place when a man and a woman promised to wed each other in front of witnesses and then had sex. So, Richard III was claiming that Edward IV had promised Eleanor Talbot that he would marry her in order to get her into bed. This scenario was not entirely implausible, as Edward IV was a bit of a rogue in his youth; however, there were some major inconsistencies that made people who were not 100% sold on Richard III doubt the validity of this claim.

1. Only one person who was apparently present at the wedding was still alive: Bishop Stillington, the man who claimed to have officiated the wedding. Edward IV was obviously dead and Eleanor herself had passed away years before.

2. Eleanor was dead before Edward V was born. So, even if the pre contract was real, Elizabeth Woodville and Edward IV could have "remarried" prior to the birth of their heir, making Edward V legitimate. As a king who was a usurper himself, why did he not take such a simple step to secure his children's inheritance?

3. Around the same time that George was executed for treason, Stillington spent some time under arrest for conspiring with George. So, if George knew that Edward IV's marriage was invalid (and remember, George hated the marriage), why did he not use this accusation instead of his more outrageous claims, such as that Elizabeth Woodville poisoned his wife, Isabella Neville (who died in childbirth).

That being said, there was a possibility that it was true. Many believed that Edward IV had only married Elizabeth Woodville because she refused to sleep with him until they were married. Plus, he had already had one secret wedding. Why not another? Also, prior to his marriage to Elizabeth Woodville, Edward

IV had met with Eleanor and there were rumors that she had given birth to his child. There was not a significant amount of evidence about whether or not she bore his child, but they definitely did meet.

Either way, Richard III presented whatever evidence that he had to the Regency Council. The same Regency Council who, days before, had witnessed Richard III execute Hastings for plotting to ensure Edward V was crowned and Richard III not continue his reign as Lord Protector, making anyone who might have objected to the evidence (or lack thereof) think twice about defending Edward V's claim. Edward IV's children by Elizabeth Woodville were unofficially declared illegitimate. It was not until months later that their bastardization was officially approved by Parliament. However, according to Richard III, Lord Protector, and his supporters, they were not eligible to inherit the throne. Richard III was now Edward IV's closest legitimate male blood relation, making him the new heir to the throne.

Elizabeth of York, the baby that once signified the beginning of a dynasty, the princess who was supposed to be the next Queen of France, was now a bastard, unable to legally inherit anything from her parents. Her once bright future was gone in an instant. Her last veil of security, as flimsy as it was, had been viciously ripped away. The crushing grief was compounded upon when, on the same day that Richard III announced her bastardry and illegally deposed her brother, his henchmen executed her uncle, Lord Rivers, and half-brother, Sir Richard Grey, who had been arrested while escorting Edward V to London. Little over a week after watching her youngest brother leave the safety of Westminster Abbey to join her other brother in the custody of their uncle, that same uncle, who promised to protect her brothers, ordered the execution of another brother and stole her inheritance. The future was looking bleak for Elizabeth of York.

Twelve

Down But Not Out

as the days pass by

the rooms get smaller

and safety is nowhere to be found.

she is running through a maze

running for her very life.

she turns the corner as

and ran straight into a wall.

E VEN TRAPPED IN THE Abbey, it was fairly easy to overhear
the latest gossip. Her mother's doctor would always bring
some juicy tidbits and the servants who ran their household
always gossiped while they were working. She spent much of her

time sitting by the window, reading one of her many treasured books. As she pretty much could recite these books in her sleep, she often used the books as cover to listen to the gossip. After all, they all assumed that she was not listening.

Today, she overheard whispers of unrest from two girls who were cleaning the apartment while her younger siblings were playing outside in the small courtyard. Apparently, Uncle Richard was having a hard time making friends. The unkind side of her considered that this was what he deserved for messing with her family, but the more charitable side of her quickly squashed those thoughts. Either way, it sounded like they may have more allies than they thought outside of the Abbey. A smile begins to spread on Elizabeth of York's face as she continues to pretend to read her book.

⋙ ⋘

For the last several years of Edward IV's reign, Richard III had been given free reign over the Northern part of England as the Constable of England. He spent these years routing out corruption and in many ways, was a man of the people. His style of rule was more "get shit done" and less "don't piss off the nobles". This worked as the Constable of England who primarily stayed in Northern England. It failed in a pretty epic way as the King of all of England. The executions of Hastings, Lord Rivers and Sir Richard Grey scared a lot of people. It was less that Richard

III got rid of his enemies; it was the way he went about getting rid of them.

These men were some of the most powerful men in England under the last king. Many saw them as untouchable; and yet, they were accused of treason and executed without being able to defend themselves or have an official trial or even significant proof that they were guilty. Hastings had even been an ally of Richard III just a month before his execution. So even though few people believed the "pre-contract" story, even die-hard Richard III supporters, people were terrified to disagree with him so soon after these executions; however, once their initial fear died down, several plans were set in motion to secure the throne for Edward IV's children.

The first uprising came about when word of Lord Rivers and Sir Richard Grey's executions spread. It was quickly squashed and Richard III used it as a justification for placing an official military barricade on Westminster Abbey. The last time that this level of security had surrounded Elizabeth of York's Sanctuary, she had watched her brother be handed over to the man who killed one brother and held two more captive. The danger was real and terrifying. While a plot to rescue her brothers was underway outside of the Abbey's walls, a scheme was being hatched within the walls for Elizabeth and her sisters to escape to France.

At this point, there was no reason for Elizabeth to believe that her family was safe in England. The King, who was her uncle, had her other uncle and half-brother killed and kept her younger brothers locked in the Tower of London. He had taken her inheritance and made her a bastard. Rendered powerless, with the walls of the Abbey closing in on her more and more each day, she watched her mother plot to get her and her sisters away from this place. The focus now became saving Edward IV's female heirs by sneaking them out of Westminster Abbey separately. Unfortunately, Richard III caught wind of this plot and tightened security around the Abbey more. Things were rapidly getting worse for Elizabeth and her family and the worst was yet to come.

Thirteen

Where, Oh Where Did the "Princes" Go?

as she turned to try another path

a wave of grief hit her

like a ton of bricks.

she drops to her knees

in the middle of the maze.

her anguished screams echoing

all around her.

THE NEWS HIT HER like a suckerpunch to the gut. Her ears began ringing and the world seemed to close in on itself.

Her little brothers might be dead. No one had seen them in weeks. She did not know how much more loss she could handle. She felt a drop of water hit her hand. She looked up at the ceiling, searching for whatever leak caused the water to fall on her, but she could not find it. She lifted her shaking hands to her cheeks, only to find that they were wet. She was crying. How long had she been crying?

While Elizabeth of York was confined to Westminster Abbey with her mother and sisters, her two younger brothers were locked away in the Tower of London, one of the most secure palaces in England (which was turned into a prison during the Tudor era). At the beginning of Richard III's coup, no one thought twice about Edward V spending the weeks leading up to his coronation in the Tower of London. It was tradition after all. When the court was in London, royalty often stayed in the Tower of London during this time period. So, it was no big deal for Edward V to stay there. Things started to get weird once his brother, Prince Richard, was brought to stay with him in the Tower until the coronation. Within days, the brothers were declared bastards. The time that they were allowed to play in the gardens kept getting reduced. Soon, their servants were not allowed to see them in person. Finally, a few months after

Richard III usurped Edward V, the brothers were seen one last time, playing in the gardens, before they seemingly disappeared.

One of the greatest unsolved mysteries of this time period in English history was what happened to Edward V and Prince Richard. They were infamously called the Princes in the Tower, despite the fact that at the time of their disappearance, they were no longer royalty and Edward V should have been a King at that point, not a Prince. Technicalities aside, the "Princes" had vanished.

Getting this news, while Richard III's army surrounded her at Westminster Abbey, was devastating for Elizabeth of York. Family was very important to Elizabeth, especially her siblings. In less than six months, she had lost her beloved father, her uncle, her half-brother, and her two younger brothers. The trauma of losing so much in such a short period of time changed Elizabeth's view of the world. She was in survival mode, concerned with safety rather than power. For a woman in medieval England, power and safety often went hand in hand.

Fourteen

The Enemy of My Enemy is My Friend

in a crowded room

she looked around

for a friendly face

or even just someone

to have the balls to make eye contact.

but not a single person

dared to look in her direction,

except for one person,

hidden in the far back corner.

꙳꙳꙳꙳꙳ ꙳꙳꙳꙳꙳

S HE WATCHED AS THE good doctor left. What they were asking of him was dangerous. Frankly, it was treason. The only other choice would be to surrender to Uncle Richard, but after the disappearance of her brothers while in his care, that did not seem like a viable option. She looked down at her mother, who was seated in the chair next to her. The woman who had always seemed larger than life looked small. The overwhelming grief of the last few months had aged her twenty years. Elizabeth of York lay her hand on her mother's shoulder and squeezed, seeking to comfort her. This was the last move that they could make to ensure their family's safety. All would be lost if this did not work.

꙳꙳꙳꙳꙳ ꙳꙳꙳꙳꙳

At the beginning of the War of the Roses, there were two factions, the Yorks and the Lancasters. By the time Elizabeth of York was a toddler, the Yorks had decimated the Lancasters. Most of the obvious Lancaster heirs were either dead or women. The remaining Lancastrian heir was the son of Margaret Beaufort, Henry Tudor, who had spent his childhood in exile while his mother continually petitioned for Edward IV to return her son's inheritance. His claim to the throne was thin as 1) it was through his mother and 2) it was from the Beaufort line, which was an illegitimate line. While he was a threat to the Yorkist reign, he was not a catastrophic one. At least he was not before the shenanigans that happened after Edward IV's death.

When Richard III took the throne, he split the Yorkist faction, severely weakening the Yorkist hold on the throne. Like a shark, Margaret Beaufort smelled blood in the water. She had spent decades playing nice with Edward IV in order to get her son's inheritance back. She had finally gotten his agreement right before his death. She was done playing nice. It was clear that the only way for Henry Tudor to return to England was for him to take the throne. She would no longer settle for just Henry Tudor's inheritance; her son was going to be king, as was his right as Henry VI's closest living legitimate male relative.

In Elizabeth Woodville, Margaret saw another mother who wanted her children safe. With this similar goal in mind, the two women began to correspond and plot to overthrow Richard III. They both had the same doctor and used him to pass letters back and forth. While very few people were allowed to enter Westminster Abbey these days, Richard III could not deny a doctor entrance to check on his patients. Elizabeth Woodville and Margaret came to an agreement; the pro-Edward V Yorkist faction would back Henry Tudor's campaign to overthrow Richard III and Henry Tudor would marry Elizabeth of York once he took the throne, making Elizabeth of York Queen of England.

This was a role that Elizabeth was definitely ready to step into. Until her brother was born, she was essentially the heir to the throne. And then, she was engaged to the future King of France, until a few years previously when Louis XI royally fucked her over. Not to mention, being Queen of England meant safety and security for Elizabeth and her family. The most traumatic moments of her life until this point were directly connected to when her parents were no longer the King and Queen of England. Despite being a daughter, as the eldest unmarried child of Edward IV, whoever she married had a claim to the throne through her, regardless of the bastardization conspiracy. It was her family's greatest political capital in this time of chaos and despair.

Unfortunately for Elizabeth, things did not pan out with this first rebellion. Buckingham, Richard III's former right hand man, had been in charge of the military until Henry Tudor arrived in England. Richard III ended up crushing Buckingham before Henry even set foot on English again for the first time in years. Defeated, Henry retreated to France, leaving his mother and Elizabeth's mother in the cross-hairs of Richard III.

Fifteen

Waltzing Into Enemy Territory

dressed all in black

she walked slowly across the Tower Green.

ghosts of days of play long gone

pass her by like whispers on the wind.

in her hands,

she holds a cloth blindfold.

she lifts it to her eyes

and ties it behind her golden head.

her hands slowly fall to her sides

as she waits,

counting her breaths.

will she die or will she live?

W ALKING INTO THE TOWER of London after leaving
Sanctuary at Westminster Abbey brought back long
forgotten memories of a happier time. For a moment, she felt
excited like she had been the last time she had left Sanctuary. Last
time, her beloved father had been waiting for her in the Tower.
Her first little brother had just been born. At the time, the worst
had been over.

This time, however, was different; the worst was just beginning.
Her father was dead. Her little brothers were missing, presumed
dead, and one of her older brothers had been executed. She was
a bastard, according to her uncle, and her future was uncertain.
The pit in her stomach seemed to sink further and further the
closer she got to the doors that led to Uncle Richard's court.
Her sisters walked a few steps behind her, following her lead.
Elizabeth of York straightened her shoulders. She had to be
strong for them. She had to protect them.

In many ways, Henry Tudor's failed invasion was Elizabeth of York's last hope of not having to deal with Uncle Richard. At least, for the time being. Elizabeth looked to her mother, Elizabeth Woodville, for what their next step would be. Unfortunately, Elizabeth Woodville was sufficiently backed into a corner. With her sons missing and presumed dead, all that was left for her was to make sure that her daughters had a future outside of the walls of Sanctuary. At this moment, the only person who could make that happen was the same man who definitely killed one of her sons (Sir Richard Grey) and was rumored to have killed her two youngest sons (Edward V and Prince Richard): Richard III.

Richard III, on the other hand, needed Elizabeth of York and her sisters out of Sanctuary yesterday. His short reign was wrought with rebellions and rumors of child murder. Every time he got rid of one rebellion, another seemed to pop up in its place. If he could get the formidable Elizabeth Woodville to release her daughters into his care, as their most powerful male relative, theoretically, some of the unrest would calm down.

For the first time since Edward IV's death, Richard III's and Elizabeth Woodville's political needs aligned. Richard III publicly swore to protect his nieces and secure marriages for them that were appropriate for their stations as Princesses of England.

With this declaration, Elizabeth of York and her sisters walked out of Sanctuary and into the care of their "loving" uncle, while their mother was sequestered away from court, in the custody of a loyal follower of Richard III.

The emergence of the former princesses did not have the affect that Richard III wanted. With his only heir's sudden death and the declining health of his wife, Anne Neville, rumors spread throughout the land, claiming that Richard III sought to make Elizabeth of York his wife, once Anne Neville died. The instigating event for these rumors seemed to be that Anne and Elizabeth attended the Christmas celebration at court, wearing a similar dress. Yes, you heard me right. Wearing matching dresses apparently equals incest. Regardless of the actual reality of Richard III and Elizabeth's relationship, these rumors were so prevalent that Richard III had to make a public declaration that he had no intention to marry his niece.

Did Elizabeth want to marry her uncle? The same man who definitely killed one brother and possibly killed two others as well? The man who declared her a bastard? Probably not. However, it would be remiss of me not to mention the Buck letter. The Buck letter was a letter found by George Buck a couple centuries after Elizabeth's death where Elizabeth, allegedly, asked one of Richard III's advisors to convince Richard III to marry her. There are a few issues with this letter.

1. The letter was only cited in George Buck's history on

Richard III and has since been lost to time. Is it possible that it did exist? Yes. But, it is also very possible that it was completely made up.

2. If the letter did exist, there was an alternative explanation. Richard III was in charge of organizing Elizabeth's marriage. He had recently married her younger sister, Cecily, to a peer well below her station. Elizabeth was in limbo, waiting for a final decision on who she would marry. She may have been asking for Richard III to just make a choice and put her out of her misery.

3. If Elizabeth did mean that she wanted to marry Richard III, it was likely motivated by love for her sisters. Later in life, she went out of her way to take care of her sisters. At this moment in her life, her family had been destroyed and the only way to protect her remaining loved ones was to get into a powerful position, such as Richard III's queen.

Regardless of whether or not either of them wanted to marry the other, the rumors was another sign of the instability of Richard III's reign. Despite being declared a illegitimate, whomever married Elizabeth of York had a claim to the throne and was a danger to Richard III. If (and it is a big IF) Richard III considered marrying Elizabeth, it was only to neutralize her power as the eldest living child of Edward IV.

Not long after Christmas, Anne passed away. Due to the rumors, Elizabeth was quickly sent away from court as Richard III began to negotiate marriages for himself and Elizabeth with Portugal. To be clear, these potential marriages were with a Portuguese princess for Richard III and a Portuguese prince for Elizabeth, not a weird incestual wedding in Portugal. Nothing ended up coming out of these negotiations as Henry Tudor invaded England.

Sixteen

Here Come the Tudors

eyes covered

she stumbled blindly

across the Tower Green.

poisonous words

floated on air around her.

she tried to turn back

to hide from what seemed to be her end

only to fall into unfamiliar arms.

ONCE AGAIN, HER FATE was in the hands of men, some of which she had never even met. The thought of how powerless she felt tasted bitter on her tongue. She angrily paced the quarters that she was given in her gilded prison. She definitely had more freedom than she did when they hid in Westminster Abbey. She had a room to herself and could go outside, after all. Nevertheless, she was confined, away from the life she once knew and the people who could change her fortune.

The most frustrating part about her situation was that she had power. Her mere presence in this world was so threatening and significant that men were currently dying over who she would marry. She was her father's heir. Whomever she married would have a claim to the English throne. And yet, Elizabeth found herself trapped, away from the people who were making the decisions about her future. She could only pray that it was the right one.

Elizabeth of York spent the remainder of RI heard III's reign isolated after she was removed from court due to the rumors surrounding her and Richard III. Despite not being present, the future of England depended on who her husband was. While Richard III was trying to neutralize her by arranging a marriage with a Portuguese prince, Henry Tudor was rallying disenchanted Yorkists against Richard III in Elizabeth's name. Many of the Lancastrians who may have supported Henry Tudor's claim to the throne had been dead and gone for years. The

Yorkists who followed him did based on the promise that he made to marry Elizabeth.

It was a race against time for Henry Tudor. If he was going to claim the throne, he needed to defeat Richard III before a marriage contract was finalized for Elizabeth. So, he rallied his troops, invaded England and defeated Richard III at the Battle of Bosworth. With the death of Richard III, Henry Tudor ended the Plantagenet dynasty, which had ruled England for centuries, and began the age of the Tudors.

Since marriage to Elizabeth was so critical to Henry's success, many expected him to rush marry her. Henry, however, proved to be much more politically savvy than anyone expected; a trait that he definitely got from his mother, Margaret Beaufort. Henry and Margaret knew that Henry's claim to the throne was shaky at best, making England ripe for rebellions. In order to rule in his own right, he had to claim the throne through right of conquest.

While England had seen its fair share of overthrown kings throughout the centuries, the usurper always justified their rebellion by claiming that they had a better claim to the throne than the current king. This was not an argument that Henry could make in his own right. So, he claimed the throne through conquest. Essentially, his argument was that he invaded England and deposed the former king and that made him the rightful king.

While this was the most solid argument he could make, it was also pretty shaky. He was able to defeat Richard III because of the Yorkist support, which had been contingent on him marrying Elizabeth. So when he did not immediately run to get hitched to Elizabeth, many of his powerful allies started to get nervous.

Seventeen

The Wedding

with shaking hands,

the young woman removes the blindfold.

the piercing sunlight

hurt her eyes.

it had been so long since

she had seen the sun.

she turns in the unfamiliar embrace,

facing the man for the first time.

THE DAY WAS FINALLY here. Butterflies filled her stomach as nerves and excitement overwhelmed her. She was getting married today! And she actually liked her future husband. She would have married anyone to get the security and safety for her family, regardless of the way he looked or the way he treated her. She felt so lucky that her future husband was handsome and they got along. She would not say that he was exceptionally kind to everyone, but he treated her well and that was all that matter. She felt the luxurious material of her gown under her fingers as she looked down at herself for the thousandth time to make sure that nothing was out of place. Her golden curls swung back and forth with every head movement. She looked up as the door creaked open, knowing that it was time.

In pure Mama's boy fashion, Henry VII ran straight to his mom, Margaret Beaufort. Now granted, it had been years since they had seen each other, but still, it was a total Mama's boy move. Henry VII got to work right away on getting his government set up. He set up his coronation and declared Richard III's major supporters traitors. Although he had not scheduled the wedding yet, he did take some steps towards preparing to marry Elizabeth. Almost immediately, Henry requested a Papal dispensation to marry Elizabeth, as they were distant cousins. Also, one of the first political actions he took was to undo Richard III's declaration that Elizabeth was a bastard. These were all necessary steps that Henry had to take to marry Elizabeth. At the same time, he did not include her in his plans for his coronation nor start to organize their wedding, which made the powerful Yorkists who backed him very nervous.

While waiting for the Papal dispensation, Elizabeth returned to court and began to get to know her future husband. While Henry was not a very demonstrative man, and never would be, Elizabeth expressed the feelings that she began to develop for her husband to the people close to her. The match was a political one, but by the time they were married, there was definitely affection between the pair. The perceived delay in solidifying their projected marriage did weigh on Elizabeth. Even the smallest hint of uncertainty regarding her marriage was terrifying. She had learned the hard way that nothing was certain and her family's future depended on her marriage.

Once they had received word that the Papal dispensation was on the way, the Yorkist faction put more pressure on Henry VII to marry Elizabeth of York as soon as possible. So finally, Henry VII married Elizabeth of York in what was the biggest royal wedding in England in several decades.

Elizabeth wore an absurd amount of jewels and an extravagant gown made of gold, purple, and crimson silk and satin. Her blonde hair was pulled back in a jewel-incorporated elaborate hairstyle. Henry was covered head to toe with gold. It seemed like the entire nation celebrated with everything from giving gifts to tournaments. Their marriage meant more than just a regular royal wedding; it symbolized the beginning of a new era and one without the years of civil war that England had just lived through.

Eighteen

A Surprising Happy Marriage

the world spins around them

round and round and round it goes

faster and faster and faster it goes

but within their bubble,

it stands still.

within their bubble,

it is safe.

within their bubble,

there is joy.

As a young girl, she wanted her husband to be like her father. Her father sucked the air out of any room he entered, in the best possible way. He was charming and outgoing. The whole court knew that he loved his wife and children dearly and demonstrated his love publicly. In her eyes, her father had been the best of men and she wanted her future husband to be the same. The man she ended up marrying was not at all like her father.

Her husband was serious in moments where her father would have made a joke. It was rare to see her husband show any emotion other than anger, especially in front of the court. The young girl that Elizabeth had once been would have hated being married to him. The woman that she had become saw beyond his steely exterior. She saw the quiet way he treated her with love behind closed doors. She saw the small sparks of humor in his eyes while he maintained a serious composure. Elizabeth looked at her husband and saw her perfect match.

England had been through the ringer when it came to the marriages of their monarchs over the last fifty or so years. Henry

VI's marriage to Margaret of Anjou was controversial as it cost England much of their French lands and she came with no dowry. Edward IV married Elizabeth Woodville in secret and many blamed Warwick's rebellion on their marriage. Richard III and Anne Neville's marriage was not super problematic; however, the fact that they only had one child and her early death did not help Richard III's reign at all.

Surprisingly, Henry VII and Elizabeth of York's marriage brought stability to the realm. They united the two warring sides of the War of the Roses. It was also a marriage that the remaining powerful English nobles desperately wanted. Beyond all of the political advantages to the marriage, the marriage itself needed to be stable.

The first few years were tough, to say the least. Henry VII delayed Elizabeth's coronation for almost twelve years for political and practical reasons. The political reasons were pretty obvious; despite being Henry VII's Queen Consort, Elizabeth's own claim to the throne was still a threat. The more time he could put between his coronation and her coronation, the better. On the other hand, the first practical reason for the delay was that Elizabeth got pregnant almost immediately. Then, the Lambert Simnel affair happened and Henry VII had to put down that rebellion. Don't worry; we will come back to that rebellion in a little bit.

Henry VII was a hard and suspicious man. The years in exile and threats of assassination due to his status as the primary Lancastrian heir shaped the way Henry viewed the world. It took a long time for Henry to really trust Elizabeth. Elizabeth, on the other hand, devoted herself to being the Queen Consort that Henry needed. She knew that her and her family's safety depended on him. Henry and their children were her first priority, which helped Henry learn to trust her.

Henry and Elizabeth spent the first few years of their marriage developing trust and affection in each other. Unlike Elizabeth's parents' marriage which was almost a love at first sight situation, the love between Henry and Elizabeth built over time. Elizabeth often traveled with Henry and they had multiple children over the years.

Nineteen

Struggles With the In-Laws

but soon enough,

the bubble burst,

letting all of their enemies in.

it is often said

those whom we love

can hurt us the most

and this was certainly true

for the new golden couple.

S HE MANAGED TO GET to her apartments before collapsing into a chair. Her chest was tight and tears sprang to her eyes. Her thoughts were whirling around in her head, so fast that she could barely process what they were. And yet, the destructive nature of the thoughts hammered at her so hard, she could feel it down to her bones. Her chest got tighter and it became harder to breathe as she considered the information that she had been given. It was possible that one of her baby brothers was alive! The news that once would have brought great joy only filled her with fear. If her brother was alive and wanted the throne, her husband was in danger. In fact, her children were in danger. The life that she had built could be gone in a minute. If it came down to it and she had to choose between her brother and her husband, she knew what she would do. There was nothing else she could do and she could only pray that God would forgive her.

Like every married couple, both Henry VII and Elizabeth of York had some major power struggles with their in-laws. The biggest hurdle for Henry were the pretenders. As there was never any confirmation about what happened to the Princes in the Tower, many people came forward throughout his reign, claiming to be one of the Princes or another relative of Elizabeth's. The Lambert Simnel affair, which was mentioned in the last chapter, was the first example of a pretender.

Lambert Simnel appeared in Ireland, claiming to be Edward Plantagenet, the only son of George, Duke of Clarence, and Isabel Neville. The irony of this rebellion was that Edward Plantagenet was imprisoned in the Tower of London. In fact, he had been imprisoned there since Henry VII had taken the throne. To disprove this, Henry paraded the real Edward Plantagenet around London before decisively putting down the rebellion that was following the Pretender. Lambert Simnel was allowed to live as it became clear that he was a scapegoat for Yorkist rebels who did not like Henry VII.

Surprisingly, it was possible that Elizabeth's mother, Elizabeth Woodville, was involved in the Lambert Simnel affair. While Henry never came right out and accused her, right after the rebellion, Henry stripped her of her titles and income and sent her to live in a convent for the rest of her life. It was possible that Elizabeth Woodville wanted to retire from court and Henry simply gave her a path to do so, but the timing was suspicious.

The other major pretender was Perkin Warbeck. Unlike Lambert Simnel, Perkin Warbeck claimed to be Prince Richard, Elizabeth's youngest brother who was one of the Princes in the Tower. Disproving that Perkin Warbeck was not Prince Richard was not as easy as dealing with Lambert Simnel. This rebellion was more significant as it was backed by Scotland and Burgundy.

Henry was able to put down this rebellion as well. To prove that Perkin was not who he claimed to be and therefore, was not a threat to his throne, Henry left Perkin alive after the rebellion. Perkin lived at court for several years before he tried to escape with Edward Plantagenet. After being recaptured, both were convicted of treason and beheaded.

While one could make the argument that Lambert and Perkin were just pretenders, so they were not officially Henry's in-laws, the same could not be said for the woman who backed both rebellions, Margaret, the former Duchess of Burgundy. Margaret, Duchess of Burgundy, was Elizabeth's aunt and had been Edward IV and Richard III's sister. She hated Henry for killing Richard III and frankly, was not a huge fan of her nieces through Edward IV, especially Elizabeth of York. She blamed the Woodvilles for the death of George, Duke of Clarence, and considered Edward IV's children to be Woodvilles.

For the most part, unlike the rest of her relatives, Elizabeth's sisters did not cause Henry much trouble. In fact, he used their marriages for his political gains and refused to financially support them. Elizabeth supported all of her sisters financially. It was not until after Elizabeth's death that any of her sisters caused Henry any problems. As a widow who felt that she had done her duty to the realm, Cecily of York married again without Henry's permission. Henry refused to acknowledge their marriage and stripped her of her inheritance from her second husband.

While many of Elizabeth's relatives (or people who claimed to be her relatives) were a pain in Henry's arse over the years, there was a constant power struggle between Elizabeth and Henry's mother, Margaret Beaufort. Margaret Beaufort was a badass. She gave birth to Henry when she was only thirteen years old. She spent years navigating English politics to get her son's inheritance returned to him. It was her political maneuvering that allowed for Henry to overthrow Richard III. The number one woman in Henry's life was Margaret Beaufort.

The Queen Consort was typically the most important woman in England during the medieval era. During Henry VII's reign, the most important woman in England was his mother. Margaret Beaufort was heavily involved in politics and did not leave any room for Elizabeth to have really any political influence. Elizabeth was certainly present and involved in court but was not involved in the politics at all.

To be fair, it was very possible that Elizabeth did not want to be involved. The biggest motivation to marry Henry and become Queen Consort was to protect herself and her family. The power and prestige was definitely a bonus, but the priority was protection. The few times that Elizabeth got involved with politics had to do with her children's betrothals. In fact, Margaret Beaufort and Elizabeth worked together to set up the betrothals. This indicates that Elizabeth had the ability to be involved when she wanted to be and the relationship between Margaret and Elizabeth was likely not as toxic as was once thought.

Twenty

Mama Elizabeth

as time went on,

through their trials and tribulations,

her belly began to grow,

with sons and daughters.

the man knelt before

and rested his forehead on large bump,

carefully cradling it with his hands.

he looked up at her,

joy filled his eyes with tears

as he whispered his gratitude.

THE QUEEN KNEW THAT many thought she was crazy for investing so much of her time and energy in teaching her children. After all, isn't that what tutors are for? But to her, this time was precious. She knew all too well that everything could go wrong in a moment and she could lose them or be separated from them. Despite how hard her husband worked to be a good King, there was civil unrest. She looks at her sons and daughters and sees herself and her siblings. In her nightmares, she sees her sons disappearing and her daughters distraught and terrified. There are many nights that she wakes up with tears running down her face.

So, she spends her days with her children. She teaches them to read and write. She watches as their eyes light up when they spell a word right or read a whole paragraph. She showers them with love like her parents did to her. Elizabeth holds her precious babies close, wanting to never let them go.

For a Queen Consort, Elizabeth was a good mother. Traditionally, royal parents did not have much to do with raising their children. For example, the heir to the throne typically left home before his tenth birthday and was raised in his own household. This was to prepare him for ruling from an early age. Elizabeth's younger brother, Edward V, had essentially been raised by their uncle, Anthony Woodville, who ran Edward V's household until Anthony's arrest and execution at the hands of Richard III. As the heir to the throne, Arthur was moved to his own household at a young age.

The one area of Arthur's life that Elizabeth was very involved in was his marriage to Katherine of Aragon. She communicated with Katherine's mother, Isabella of Castille, and Katherine herself in preparation of her arrival in England.

On the other hand, Elizabeth was able to take a much more hands-on approach with his siblings, especially the future Henry VIII. The main lesson that Elizabeth learned throughout all of the upheaval in her life was that family was everything. Much like her mother tried to do, Elizabeth devoted her life to making sure her children had the best lives possible. The first teacher that most of her children had was Elizabeth herself. She taught them how to write and read before they began their official tutoring. She was involved in their everyday lives, unless her other duties as Queen Consort got in the way.

Another example of Elizabeth as a mother was when Elizabeth teamed up with her mother-in-law, Margaret Beaufort, to advocate for her oldest daughter, Princess Margaret. She was engaged to James IV, the King of Scotland, at a very young age. Typically, even if the future wife was below the age of consent, after the solidification of the betrothal, the wife was sent to live with her betrothed's family. While this may seem super gross, there were some practical reasons behind doing this. It allowed for the wife to learn the customs of her betrothed as well as what her responsibilities would be within the household after their marriage. It would also allow the couple to get to know each other and build a friendship prior to marriage.

The concern that both Elizabeth and Margaret Beaufort had was that James IV would attempt to consummate the marriage to Princess Margaret too early. Margaret Beaufort herself had been a victim of this. Her first husband, Edmund Tudor, had consummated their marriage when Margaret Beaufort was only twelve years old. She became pregnant almost immediately and the birth almost killed both Margaret Beaufort and her son, Henry VII, who would end up being her only child. As much as she loved her son, she did not want her granddaughter to suffer the way that she did. Together, Elizabeth and Margaret Beaufort were able to convince Henry VII that Princess Margaret would marry James IV by proxy but would not move to Scotland until she was older.

Twenty-One

The Death of Prince Arthur

but, of course,

it cannot just be

all sunshine and roses.

heaven knows bliss is not meant to last.

the cruelest fate

steals away her first baby,

her pride and joy,

the future of her dynasty.

S HE KNEW SOMETHING WAS wrong the minute that he
walked through the door. Her husband rarely showed any
emotion and she could see the tears in his eyes, even from far
away. Something had clearly happened to one of their loved
ones. Time slowed as she pieced together the horrible news. It
was not her sisters, as while he knew she would be upset, he
would not be. He seemed to expect her to be distraught, so it
was unlikely that it was his mother. The world seemed to drop
out from under Elizabeth as she realized that the only ones left
were their children.

While Arthur was not the first of their children to pass away
(as two of their children died before the age of 5), his death,
due to illness, had the most profound impact on both Elizabeth
of York and Henry VII. While he had spent much of his short
life separated from his parents, Arthur had been their first child
and had represented the bright future of the Tudor dynasty.
Their absolute devastation at the loss provided a rare glimpse
into what their marriage looked like behind closed doors.

After receiving the news of Arthur's death, Henry immediately went to Elizabeth. While telling her what happened, the
normally stoic Henry broke down. Elizabeth comforted him
the best she could. Once he regained his composure, he left
her with her ladies. Once he was out of the room, she became

inconsolable. When word got to Henry of Elizabeth's state, he stopped what he was doing and went to her side, comforting her much in the same way that she had comforted him moments before.

While this may not seem like a grand show of affection, for Elizabeth and Henry, it was. Henry was known to be almost unfeeling and solely focused on ruling England. The fact that he became so distraught demonstrated how much he did care for his family. Furthermore, to stop what he was doing and immediately go to Elizabeth's side showed how precious she was to him. The death of the heir to throne had significant political impacts, but Henry's first priority in that moment was to grieve for his son with his wife. He decided to deal with the political and practical arrangements that needed to be made with Arthur's death later. Elizabeth came first.

Twenty-Two

More Tragedy for the Tudors

her arms felt empty.

the hole in her heart

ached with every breath.

desperate to fix what was broken,

she made a choice

that would destroy everything.

She cradled her pregnant belly as a tear rolled down her cheek. This should be a joyful time but there was only pain and sorrow. With only one heir and no spare, there was no other option but to have another child. She felt her child's soft kicks against her hands. They were weaker than they should be at this stage. Nothing about this as going the way that it was supposed. She was in pain and tired. She tried to put on a brave face for her children and husband, but knew that her husband could see through it. Elizabeth knew in her bones that something was not right. All she could do was pray.

Elizabeth of York's last pregnancy prior to Arthur's death had not gone well. It had been a hard birth and the baby, Edmund, had not lived to see his first birthday. With two sons and two daughters, the Tudor dynasty was secure and for the sake of her health, Henry and Elizabeth stopped trying to have children. The death of Arthur changed things. With only one male heir, the pressure was on to produce another son. So they started trying again and soon enough, Elizabeth was pregnant again.

This pregnancy did not go well. Elizabeth went into labor well before her due date. In fact, she had not even entered into her confinement. Confinement was when noble women went into seclusion for the last few weeks of their pregnancy. They typically had some female relatives with them and a midwife but were confined to a room or set of rooms. It was kind of like what we call bedrest.

Elizabeth had planned to spend her confinement at Richmond Castle. The preparations were already being made when she traveled to the Tower of London with Henry VII. While at the Tower, Elizabeth went into premature labor. She gave birth to a daughter named Katherine. Unfortunately, Katherine died while still in infancy. This labor was hard on Elizabeth. A week after giving birth, her health took a turn for the worse. With Henry VII by her side, she passed away on her birthday at the age of thirty seven.

Twenty-Three

The Legacy of Elizabeth of York

the golden princess

became a golden queen.

kind and joyous,

she was loved by all.

her country mourned her.

her children cried for her.

her grandchildren were named for her.

The Queen Who Should Have Been The First.

THE ENTIRE NATION OF England was devastated at the loss of Elizabeth of York. She had been the embodiment of a good medieval queen consort and was beloved by the people. Her children desperately missed her. The person who had demonstrated how profoundly her loss affected him was surprisingly Henry VII.

Elizabeth and Henry had never been a couple who engaged in any form of PDA. They kept the inner workings of their marriage very private. After her death, however, there was a marked change in Henry. While he had never been considered benevolent, he became much colder and harsher in the last years of his reign. Despite having options and only having one male heir, he never remarried. He did make one significant change that had many ripple effects that not even he could have predicted.

Prior to Elizabeth's death, the Tower of London was one of most used Royal Palaces. All the monarchs stayed in the Tower prior to their coronation. It was the most secure place in London for the royal family to reside. In fact, it had been one of Edward IV's favorite palaces and Elizabeth had spent much of her childhood there. The disappearance of her brothers definitely tainted the Tower for her, but Henry and Elizabeth spent time there throughout their reign. It was only after her death that Henry decided that he would no longer use the Tower as a royal residence. The Tower became the place to hold political prisoners and for the executions of nobility. Some of the nobles who were executed at the Tower were Anne Boleyn and Katherine Howard, two of Elizabeth's own daughter-in-laws.

Beyond the direct aftermath of her death, Elizabeth's impact on England through the next several decades. The son that she had a significant hand in raising, Henry VIII, became the next King of England. He viewed his mother as the ideal queen and his parents' marriage as the ideal marriage, to the detriment of his future wives. The only wife that he felt was comparable to Elizabeth was Jane Seymour. Jane was the only wife to give him a son and like his mother, she died in childbirth. Her funeral was fashioned after Elizabeth's own funeral, linking Jane to Elizabeth decades after her death.

Elizabeth of York's death also destabilized Henry VII's rule. Despite staying relatively out of politics for her reign as Queen of England, many still viewed her as the rightful heir to the throne. By this logic, Henry VIII, as her only living male heir, should have been crowned king upon Elizabeth's death. Her husband, Henry VII, became so paranoid that his enemies would take advantage of his teenage son and try to overthrow Henry VII in his son's name, that he barely let Henry VIII out of his sight until his death.

The legacy of Elizabeth of York's stolen claim to the throne lasted well beyond even her husband's death and her son's rise to the throne. Henry VIII's claim to the throne was often referenced as though it came from his mother's side of the family. He named his only son Edward after his grandfather on his mother's side instead of Henry like himself and his father. This was to tie his son's right to rule to his mother's superior claim to the throne. This was not the first time Henry VIII utilized a connection to his mother to solidify his dynasty's right to rule.

Henry VIII pretty much lived on the struggle bus when it came to securing his heir. He married Katherine of Aragon as a teenager and after two decades of trying, only had one living legitimate child, Mary. Desperate to get a male heir, he broke from the Catholic Church when the pope refused to annul his marriage. As a way to legitimize his very controversial marriage to Anne Boleyn, he named their only living child Elizabeth after his mother. This was a huge statement. By naming the child Elizabeth, he was declaring that she was the legitimate heir, much like her namesake, Elizabeth of York. But, her legacy went beyond her claim to the throne.

There was no question that Elizabeth of York's marriage to Henry VII was a political one. Their marriage certainly became a very loving one over the years, but it did not start out that way. Their children, Henry VIII, Mary and Margaret, only saw how loving their relationship was at the end rather than how it came about. This led to each of them having some marital blunders. Henry VIII ended up having six separate wives, two of which he beheaded. Mary pulled a Woodville and after her first husband died, she married for love without permission from Henry VIII.

Margaret's first marriage was a successful political one to the King of Scotland, but her next two marriages ended on not so great terms.

All in all, for a queen who is often overlooked, Elizabeth of York's impact was felt for decades after her death.

Epilogue: The Snarky Poem of Elizabeth of York

the nation held their breath
in the deep dark of the night
waiting...
waiting...
waiting...
"the Queen is in labor"
was the whisper on the wind.
"is it a boy or a girl?"
a pit grows in the stomach of the nation
as the night seems endless.
bright light suddenly bursts through
as word spreads
of the birth of the new heir,
Princess Elizabeth.

a political pawn,

even at the tender age of four.

her hand in marriage

treated as a consolation prize,

given to whomever whines the loudest.

the loudest lord of them all,

the man who slaughtered her family

wins the prize...

at least for today.

all at once,

everything changed.

the world that was once so big

shrunk to three borrowed rooms.

everything was taken away

all at once.

her knight in shining armor

came back to save the day

riding in on his white steed.

it was easy to ignore

the stains of blood

that he tried to wash away

when the shining light of freedom

hit her eyes once more.

her daddy came home

and everything would be okay...

but was it really all hunky dory dory?

were all the villains of this story

washed away with

the blood of Teweksbury?

nah.

King Eddie stuck his head in the sand

as Uncle Georgie Porgie danced on graves;

cackling in the moonlight.

the golden princess

is to be the next Queen of France,

as long as fickle foes stay true.

but alas, they rarely do.

the Princess may be the Dauphine for now,

but a better offer may come through.

with the removal

of one single card,

the Tower of Cards

that the princess lives in

comes crashing

down

down

down.

her world shrunk

from palaces and parties

to a few rooms and prayers.

so familiar but yet so foreign.

the wails that echoed through the rooms

had once upon a time belonged to her brother

now emerged from her mother.

there would be no white knight this time.

there would be no hope this time.

the countdown to the big day begins.

the coronation should be the event of the decade.

freedom seems so close

yet so far away.

dark rumblings bubble up

From below the surface.

a volcano of chaos began to erupt.

lava slowly dripping down the side of the mountain,

inching closer and closer.

"Uncle" Hastings was the first

taken by the lava

Uncle Anthony and Older Richard were next.

she watched, helpless, as

the stranger who was her uncle

escorted her baby brother

up the mountain

towards the lava.

he used treachery

when he came for the Woodvilles.

he used his authority

when he came for "Uncle" Hastings.

he used his army

when he came for her brother.

there was no one left to protect her

when they came for her name.

as the days pass by

the rooms get smaller

and safety is nowhere to be found.

she is running through a maze

running for her very life.

she turns the corner as

and ran straight into a wall.

as she turned to try another path

a wave of grief hit her

like a ton of bricks.

she drops to her knees

in the middle of the maze.

her anguished screams echoing

all around her.

in a crowded room

she looked around

for a friendly face

or even just someone

to have the balls to make eye contact.

but not a single person

dared to look in her direction,

except for one person,

hidden in the far back corner.

dressed all in black

she walked slowly across the Tower Green.

ghosts of days of play long gone

pass her by like whispers on the wind.

in her hands,

she holds a cloth blindfold.

she lifts it to her eyes

and ties it behind her golden head.

her hands slowly fall to her sides

as she waits,

counting her breaths.

will she die or will she live?

eyes covered

she stumbled blindly

across the Tower Green.

poisonous words

floated on air around her.

she tried to turn back

to hide from what seemed to be her end

only to fall into unfamiliar arms.

with shaking hands,

the young woman removes the blindfold.

the piercing sunlight

hurt her eyes.

it had been so long since

she had seen the sun.

she turns in the unfamiliar embrace,

facing the man for the first time.

the world spins around them

round and round and round it goes

faster and faster and faster it goes

but within their bubble,

it stands still.

within their bubble,

it is safe.

within their bubble,

there is joy.

but soon enough,

the bubble burst,

letting all of their enemies in.

it is often said

those whom we love

can hurt us the most

and this was certainly true

for the new golden couple.

as time went on,

through their trials and tribulations,

her belly began to grow,

with sons and daughters.

the man knelt before

and rested his forehead on large bump,

carefully cradling it with his hands.

he looked up at her,

joy filled his eyes with tears

as he whispered his gratitude.

but, of course,

it cannot just be

all sunshine and roses.

heaven knows bliss is not meant to last.

the cruelest fate

steals away her first baby,

her pride and joy,

the future of her dynasty.

her arms felt empty.

the hole in her heart

ached with every breath.

desperate to fix what was broken,

she made a choice

that would destroy everything.

the golden princess

became a golden queen.

kind and joyous,

she was loved by all.

her country mourned her.

her children cried for her.

her grandchildren were named for her.

The Queen Who Should Have Been The First.

Appendix A: Sources and Further Reading

Amin, Nathen. *Henry VII and the Tudor Pretenders: Simnel, Warbeck, Warwick.* Amberley Publishing. Gloucestershire: 2020. Kindle Edition.

Gristwood, Sarah. *Blood Sisters: The Women Behind the Wars of the Roses.* Basic Books. New York: 2013. Kindle Edition.

Hilton, Lisa. *Queens Consort: England's Medieval Queens from Eleanor of Aquitaine to Elizabeth of York.* Pegasus Books. New York: 2021. Kindle Edition.

Acknowledgements

Thank you to my amazing and supportive parents for editing this piece and for being my biggest support.

Thank you to my siblings who always have my back (except when we are playing any game. Then it is every man for themselves).

Thank you to my Bride Day Friday gals for cheering me on.

Thank you to Dodo for being my cover design sounding board.

Thank you to Jersey for indulging my sweet tooth with your amazing baked goods.

Thank you to Margaret Megan for reminding me what the important things in life are.

Most of all, thank you to all of my friends and family who dealt with my crazy while I made this happen. I could not have done this without all of you.

About the Author

About the Author

K. Lee Pelt, otherwise known as "the Snarky History Nerd", fell in love with stories at a young age. She was always reading and coming up with stories in her head. As she got older, the love of stories expanded to a love of history, which, in many ways, is one giant story from many different perspectives. After completing her Bachelor of Arts in Medieval European History, she went on to get a Masters of Education. K. Lee utilizes her degrees to tell the stories of history, especially those of women, with a snarky twist.

When she is not writing, you can find K. Lee watching TV (usually some form of comedy or snarky drama) or reading everything from fanfiction to history books to romance novels with her cat, Noelle, climbing all over her.

Also By K. Lee Pelt

Catherine of Valois: The Tudor Queen Ahead of Her Time

Dutiful Princess. Ideal Queen Consort. Doting Queen Mother. Defiant Queen Dowager.

Catherine of Valois spent the majority of her life doing exactly what was expected of her. She married the English King Henry V as part of a treaty to end the Hundred Years' War. She gave him a son almost immediately. But when he died and her brothers-in-law booted her off of the throne, she finally had enough. She found her happiness and took it, regardless of the consequences. These actions led directly to the rise of England's most notorious dynasty, the Tudors.

Find out more about the English Queen who brought the best dowry and directly defied a royal decree to marry the man that she wanted. She was instrumental in both the Hundred Years War and the War of the Roses; two critical events that shaped Medieval England and medieval history as a whole.

Available Now on Amazon.

Note from the Author

Thank you so much for taking the time to read about this amazing English Queen Consort, Elizabeth of York. I hope you enjoyed reading it.

I would greatly appreciate it if you would:

Review this book. This helps authors immensely. So if you liked this book and are willing to, please submit a review on Amazon.

Share this book: If you like this book, please share it with your friends, either in person or across social media. This will help tremendously.

Connect with me: I would love to chat with anyone about Medieval history. You can email me at <u>thesnarkyhistorynerd@gmail.com</u> or connect with me through social media. My social media information is in the "Stay Tuned..." Section.

ELIZABETH OF YORK

Stay Tuned...

The next book in the works is on Margaret Beaufort, Elizabeth of York's mother-in-law and the woman who made the Tudor dynasty a reality. You can keep up to date on all things Snarky History Nerd, including release dates and blog posts, by following me on social media or checking out my website. The details are below:

Website: snarkyhistorynerd.com

TikTok: @kleepeltsnarkyhistory

Twitter: @snarky_history

Instagram: snarkyhistorynerd

Facebook Page: https://m.facebook.com/100086266522638/

Printed in Great Britain
by Amazon

26738142R00075